Classroom Rules

Betsy Franco
Photographs by Ken O'Donoghue

HOUGHTON MIFFLIN HARCOURT

www.Rigby.com
800-531-5015

We have classroom rules.
Rules help us and
keep us safe.

Classroom Rules

Rule 1: Share.

Rule 2: Be a helper.

Rule 3: Talk about it.

Rule 4: Put up your hand to talk.

Rule 5: Take turns.

Rule 1: Share.

We all want to use
the new box of crayons.
We know what to do.
We can share the crayons!

Classroom Rules

Rule 1: Share.
Rule 2: Be a helper.
Rule 3: Talk about it.
Rule 4: Put up your hand to ta
Rule 5: Take turns.

I Looked Through My Window

Michaela Morgan
Illustrated by Anthony Lewis

5

Rule 2: Be a helper.

Our teacher needs
to pass out papers.
There are so many papers!
We can pass out the papers
to help the teacher.

Classroom Rules

Rule 1: Share.

Rule 2: Be a helper.

Rule 3: Talk about it.

Rule 4: Put up your hand to talk.

Rule 5: Take turns.

I Looked Through My Window

7

Rule 3: Talk about it.

Jill broke Rafi's pencil.
Rafi is mad.

Jill and Rafi don't hit and shout.
They talk about it.
Jill gives Rafi one of her pencils.

Rule 4: Put up your hand to talk.

Carmen wants to say something.
What should she do?
She puts up her hand.
Then the teacher will let her talk.

13

Rule 5: Take turns.

We are playing
with the class pet.
Everyone wants to give him food.
We don't grab or push.
We take turns and
have more fun that way.

15

Now you know
our classroom rules.
Rules help us,
and rules keep us safe!

Classroom Rules

Rule 1: Share.

Rule 2: Be a helper.

Rule 3: Talk about it.

Rule 4: Put up your hand to talk.

Rule 5: Take turns.